CRISTIANO RONALDO

SPORTS SUPERSTARS

BY GOLRIZ GOLKAR

BELLWETHER MEDIA · MINNEAPOLIS, MN

Torque brims with excitement perfect for thrill-seekers of all kinds. Discover daring survival skills, explore uncharted worlds, and marvel at mighty engines and extreme sports. In *Torque* books, anything can happen. Are you ready?

This edition first published in 2024 by Bellwether Media, Inc.

No part of this publication may be reproduced in whole or in part without written permission of the publisher. For information regarding permission, write to Bellwether Media, Inc., Attention: Permissions Department, 6012 Blue Circle Drive, Minnetonka, MN 55343.

Library of Congress Cataloging-in-Publication Data

Names: Golkar, Golriz, author.
Title: Cristiano Ronaldo / by Golriz Golkar.
Description: Minneapolis, MN : Bellwether Media, 2024. | Series: Sports superstars | Includes bibliographical references and index. | Audience: Ages 7-12 | Audience: Grades 4-6 | Summary: "Engaging images accompany information about Cristiano Ronaldo. The combination of high-interest subject matter and light text is intended for students in grades 3 through 7"– Provided by publisher.
Identifiers: LCCN 2023006479 (print) | LCCN 2023006480 (ebook) | ISBN 9798886874631 (library binding) | ISBN 9798886876512 (ebook)
Subjects: LCSH: Ronaldo, Cristiano, 1985–Juvenile literature. | Soccer players–Portugal–Biography–Juvenile literature.
Classification: LCC GV942.7.R626 G65 2024 (print) | LCC GV942.7.R626 (ebook) | DDC 796.334092 [B]–dc23/eng/20230213
LC record available at https://lccn.loc.gov/2023006479
LC ebook record available at https://lccn.loc.gov/2023006480

Text copyright © 2024 by Bellwether Media, Inc. TORQUE and associated logos are trademarks and/or registered trademarks of Bellwether Media, Inc.

Editor: Rachael Barnes   Designer: Gabriel Hilger

Printed in the United States of America, North Mankato, MN.

TABLE OF CONTENTS

GOAL!	4
WHO IS CRISTIANO RONALDO?	6
A RISING STAR	8
SOCCER SUPERSTAR	12
CR7'S FUTURE	20
GLOSSARY	22
TO LEARN MORE	23
INDEX	24

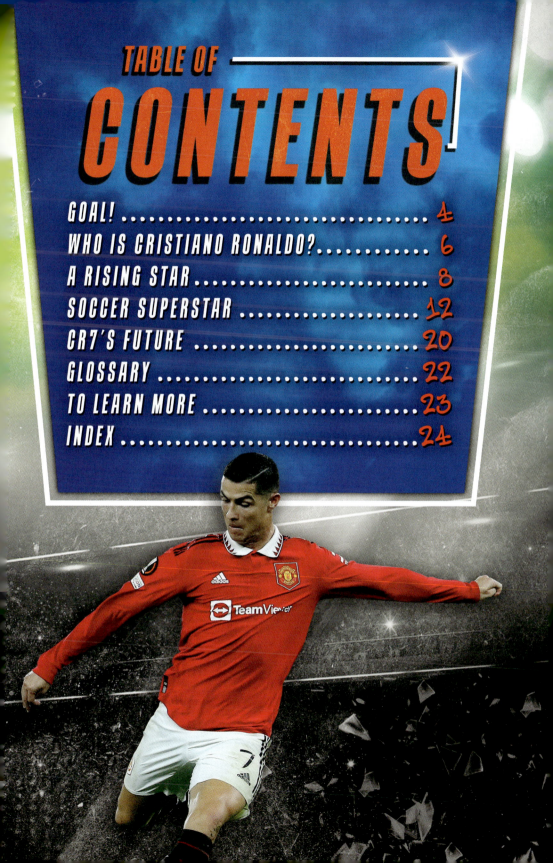

GOAL!

It is the last game of the 2017 **Champions League**. Cristiano Ronaldo's team, Real Madrid, is leading 2–1 over Juventus. Ronaldo and his teammates control the ball. Modrić passes to Ronaldo. In a flash, Ronaldo shoots the ball into the net. Ronaldo scores!

Real Madrid goes on to win 4–1. Ronaldo wins his fourth Champions League **title**!

CR7

Ronaldo's nickname is CR7. It combines his initials and his most common uniform number.

WHO IS CRISTIANO RONALDO?

Cristiano Ronaldo is a soccer player. He is a **forward**. He has played for many popular teams. He has scored more **goals** in **international** games than any other male soccer player in the world!

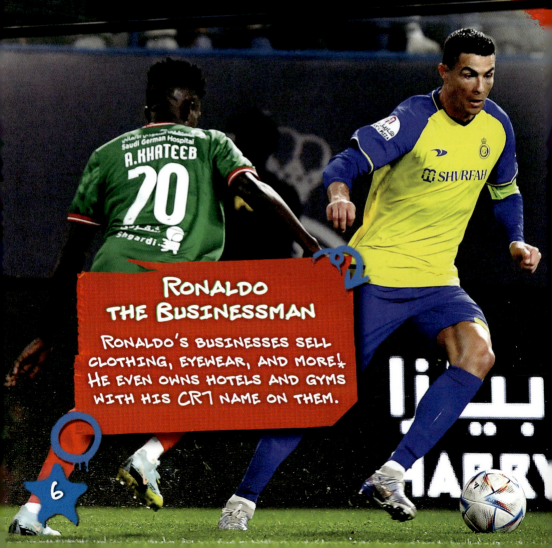

Ronaldo the Businessman

Ronaldo's businesses sell clothing, eyewear, and more!* He even owns hotels and gyms with his CR7 name on them.

CRISTIANO RONALDO

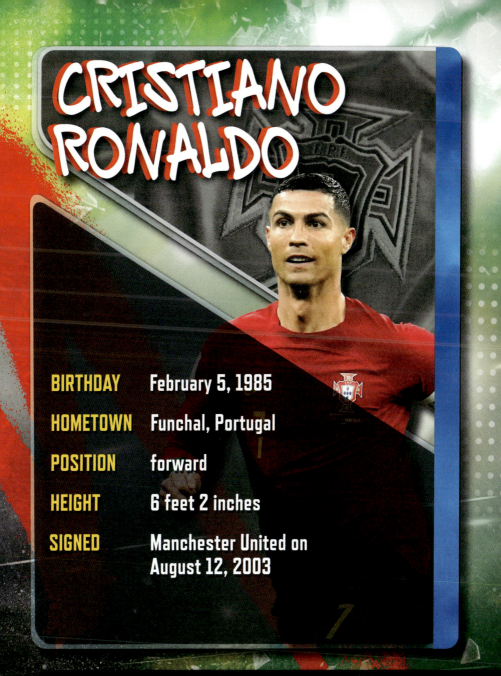

BIRTHDAY	February 5, 1985
HOMETOWN	Funchal, Portugal
POSITION	forward
HEIGHT	6 feet 2 inches
SIGNED	Manchester United on August 12, 2003

Ronaldo owns several companies. He works with Nike and other businesses. He is also a **philanthropist**. He gives his time and money to help people in need.

A RISING STAR

Ronaldo grew up in Portugal with his family. His father worked at a soccer **club**. Ronaldo visited him to play soccer for fun.

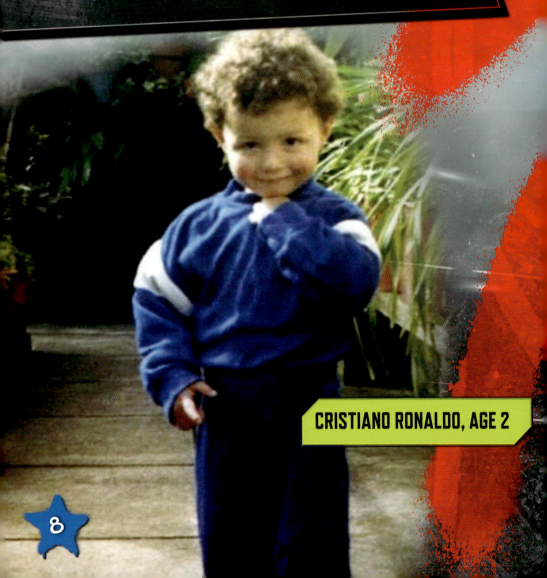

CRISTIANO RONALDO, AGE 2

RONALDO WITH FAMILY AND FRIENDS

From a young age, Ronaldo played on local soccer teams. A **scout** for Portugal's top soccer school, Sporting CP, noticed his talent. Ronaldo was asked to join the school in Lisbon, Portugal. He agreed and moved away from home at age 11.

When he was 15 years old, Ronaldo learned he had a heart problem. He needed **surgery**. It was a success. He could play soccer again! He was soon a top player for Sporting CP. He joined the senior team in 2002.

Many famous soccer teams wanted Ronaldo to play for them. In 2003, he decided to join Manchester United in England.

FAVORITES

HOBBY	FOOD	COLOR	ANIMAL
bingo	fish	white	dog

RONALDO SIGNING WITH MANCHESTER UNITED

SOCCER SUPERSTAR

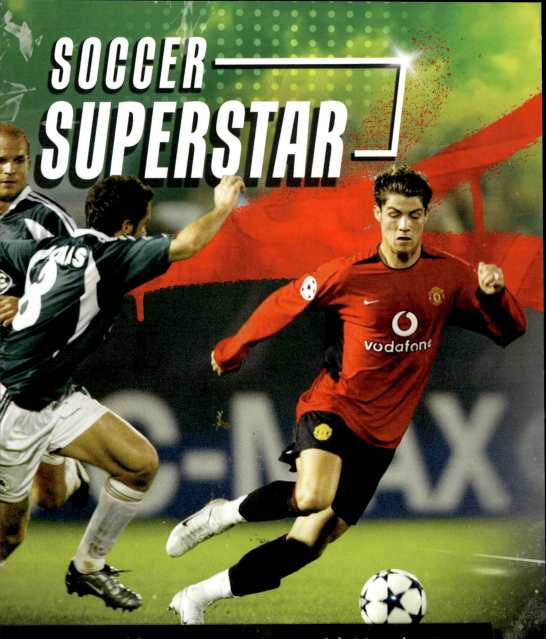

Ronaldo was a young star with Manchester United. The 18-year-old scored six goals during his first season! Ronaldo got better each season. He scored even more goals. He became famous for long distance **free kicks**.

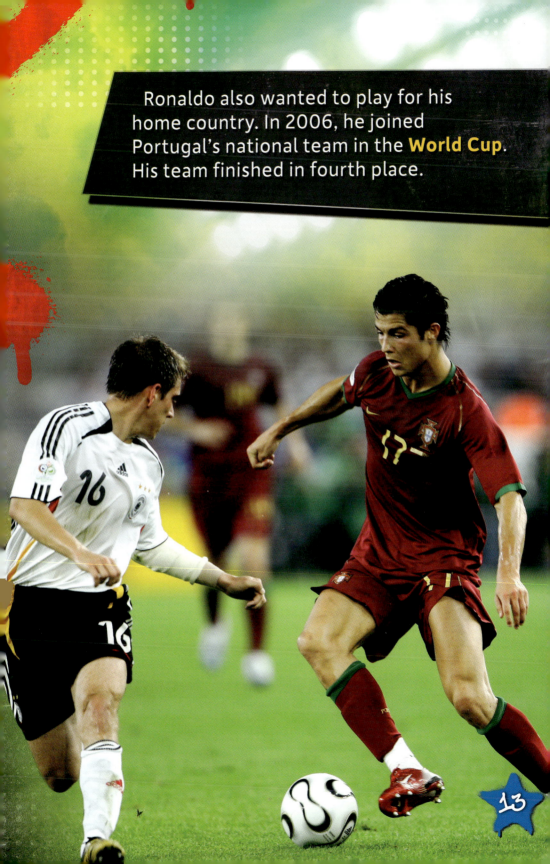

Ronaldo also wanted to play for his home country. In 2006, he joined Portugal's national team in the **World Cup**. His team finished in fourth place.

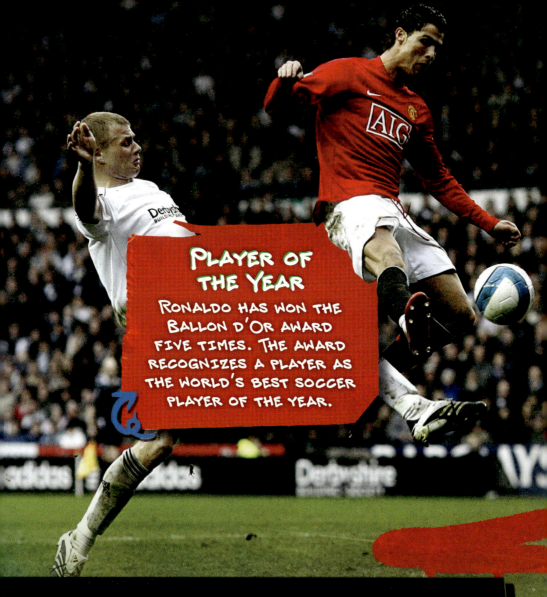

Player of the Year

Ronaldo has won the Ballon d'Or award five times. The award recognizes a player as the world's best soccer player of the year.

During the 2007–2008 season, Ronaldo scored 42 goals. He helped Manchester United win the Champions League title again after nine years.

In 2008, Ronaldo won his first Ballon d'Or award. He was also the season's top goal scorer in Europe!

CRISTIANO RONALDO MAP

- **Manchester United, Manchester, England** — 2003 to 2009, 2021 to 2022
- **Real Madrid, Madrid, Spain** — 2009 to 2018
- **Juventus, Turin, Italy** — 2018 to 2021
- **Portuguese National Team, Oeiras, Portugal** — 2006 to 2022
- **Al Nassr, Riyadh, Saudi Arabia** — 2023 to present

BALLON D'OR AWARD

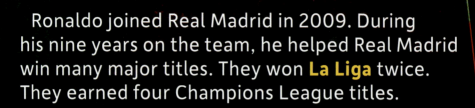

Ronaldo joined Real Madrid in 2009. During his nine years on the team, he helped Real Madrid win many major titles. They won **La Liga** twice. They earned four Champions League titles.

In 2015, Ronaldo became Real Madrid's all-time goal scorer! Ronaldo played for Portugal again in the 2018 World Cup. That July, he left Real Madrid to play for Juventus.

2018 WORLD CUP

TROPHY SHELF

Ballon d'Or winner

UEFA Best Player in Europe

Champions League winner

FIFA Club World Cup winner

La Liga winner

17

Ronaldo and Juventus won three Italian **championships**. In 2019, he became the first soccer player to win championships in the top English, Spanish, and Italian **leagues**.

In 2021, Ronaldo signed a deal to return to Manchester United for two years. He scored his 700th goal in club soccer while playing for them!

TIMELINE

— 2003 —
Ronaldo joins Manchester United

— 2008 —
Ronaldo wins his first Champions League title

— 2009 —
Ronaldo joins Real Madrid

FIFA Club World Cup Winner

The FIFA Club World Cup happens once every year. Winning teams from soccer leagues around the world play against each other. Ronaldo has won four major awards in this contest!

— 2018 —
Ronaldo joins Juventus

— 2021 —
Ronaldo returns to Manchester United

— 2023 —
Ronaldo joins Al Nassr

CR7'S FUTURE

In 2022, Ronaldo played for Portugal in the World Cup. They lost to Morocco in the **quarterfinals**. Soon after, he joined a new team. He moved to Saudi Arabia to play for Al Nassr.

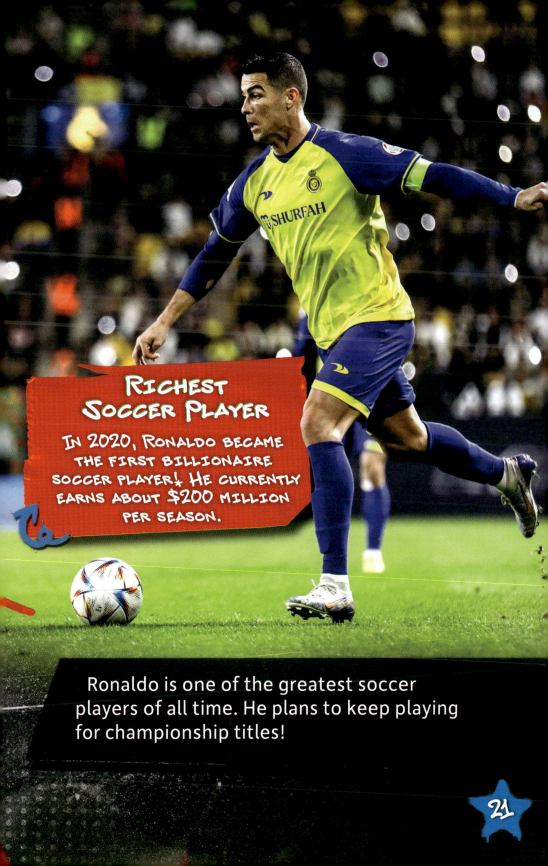

Richest Soccer Player

In 2020, Ronaldo became the first billionaire soccer player! He currently earns about $200 million per season.

Ronaldo is one of the greatest soccer players of all time. He plans to keep playing for championship titles!

GLOSSARY

Champions League—a European soccer tournament where the winners of top European leagues play each other to decide the best team in Europe

championships—contests to decide the best team or person

club—a soccer program that players advance through

forward—a position in soccer that involves trying to score or help teammates score goals

free kicks—kicks to restart the game made by a player who has been fouled

goals—points in soccer

international—involving two or more countries

La Liga—Spain's top men's soccer league

leagues—large groups of sports teams that often play each other

philanthropist—a person who works to help other people

quarterfinals—one of four games in a contest that decides who plays in the semifinals

scout—a person who watches players in action and recommends them for a team

surgery—an operation to heal an injury or treat a disease

title—a championship win

World Cup—an international soccer tournament held every four years

TO LEARN MORE

AT THE LIBRARY

Bolte, Mari. *FIFA*. North Mankato, Minn.: Norwood House Press, 2023.

Rustad, Martha E.H. *What You Never Knew About Cristiano Ronaldo*. North Mankato, Minn.: Capstone, 2023.

Stabler, David. *Meet Cristiano Ronaldo*. Minneapolis, Minn.: Lerner Publications, 2023.

ON THE WEB

FACTSURFER

Factsurfer.com gives you a safe, fun way to find more information.

1. Go to www.factsurfer.com

2. Enter "Cristiano Ronaldo" into the search box and click 🔍.

3. Select your book cover to see a list of related content.

INDEX

Al Nassr, 20
awards, 4, 14, 15, 19
Ballon d'Or, 14, 15
billionaire, 21
businesses, 6, 7
Champions League, 4, 14, 16
championships, 18, 21
childhood, 8, 9, 10
club, 8, 18, 19
England, 10, 18
family, 8, 9
favorites, 11
FIFA Club World Cup, 19
forward, 6
free kicks, 12
goals, 4, 6, 12, 14, 16, 18

Juventus, 4, 16, 18
La Liga, 16
Manchester United, 10, 11, 12, 14, 18
map, 15
nickname, 5, 6
number, 5
Portugal, 8, 9, 13, 16, 20
profile, 7
Real Madrid, 4, 16
Saudi Arabia, 20
Sporting CP, 9, 10
surgery, 10
timeline, 18–19
title, 4, 14, 16, 21
trophy shelf, 17
World Cup, 13, 16, 17, 20

The images in this book are reproduced through the courtesy of: Yasser Bakhsh/ Stringer/ Getty Images, front cover; Stefan Constantin 22, p. 3; Angel Martinez - Real Madrid/ Contributor/ Getty Images, p. 4; Jonathan Moscrop/ Contributor/ Getty Images, pp. 4-5; STR/ AP Images, pp. 6-7; Alessandra Tarantino/ AP Images, p. 7; Charnsitr, p. 7 (Portugal national soccer team logo); ARCHIVIO GBB/ Alamy, p. 8; REUTERS/ Alamy, p. 9; Icon Sport/ Contributor/ Getty Images, p. 10; John Peters/ Contributor/ Getty Images, pp. 11, 15 (Ballon d'Or award); Mega Pixel, p. 11 (bingo); Nata Bene, p. 11 (fish); Elena11, p. 11 (white); Dmitry Kalinovsky, p. 11 (dog); Ross Kinnaird/ Staff/ Getty Images, p. 12; Vladimir Rys/ Staff/ Getty Images, p. 13; Dave Thompson/ AP Images, pp. 14-15; PhotoLondonUK, p. 15 (Manchester, Madrid); MikeDotta, p. 15 (Turin); Xinovap, p. 15 (Portugal); Alina.chiorean, p. 15 (Riyadh); Andres Kudacki/ AP Images, pp. 16-17; Zhong zhenbin/ ICHPL Imaginechina/ AP Images, p. 17; Alberto Gandolfo/ Sipa USA via AP Images, p. 18; Raffaele1, p. 18 (Manchester United logo, Real Madrid logo); Alberto Gandolfo/ Sipa USA via AP/ AP Images, pp. 18-19; Valerio Pennicino - Juventus FC/ Contributor/ Getty Images, p. 19 (2018); Kamil Taran, p. 19 (Al Nassr logo); Petr David Josek/ AP Images, p. 20; Anadolu Agency/ Contributor/ Getty Images, p. 21; sportoakimirka, p. 23.